Key Note Recognition

by
Bruce Arnold

Muse Eek Publishing Company
New York, New York

ISBN 1-890944-77-7

Printed in the United States

This publication can be purchased from your local bookstore or by contacting:
Muse Eek Publishing Company
P.O. Box 509
New York, NY 10276, USA
Phone: 212-473-7030
Fax: 212-473-4601
http://www.muse-eek.com
sales@muse-eek.com

Table Of Contents

Acknowledgments

The author would like to thank Michal Shapiro for proof reading and helpful suggestions. I would also like to thank my students who through their questions helped me to see their needs so that I might address them as best I could.

About the Author

Bruce Arnold is a guitarist, composer, educator, and author. As a musician, he has achieved a sound that sets him apart by applying jazz improvisational techniques to 20th century-12-tone compositional methods. He has recorded three critically acclaimed CDs that document his unique approach to composition and improvisation, and he has also pioneered the use of the guitar as a controller via the computer program SuperCollider. Bruce co-leads the group Spooky Actions which takes music from sources as far afield as Native American songs to classics by composers such as Webern and Messiaen as vehicles for improvisation. Bruce has a distinguished and versatile performance history, having performed with Stanley Clarke, Joe Pass, Joe Lovano, Randy Brecker, Peter Erskine, Stuart Hamm, the Absolute Ensemble under the baton of Kristjan Järvi,and the Boston Symphony Orchestra. He is the author of over 50 books on music education and directs the groundbreaking NYU Summer Guitar Intensive, which annually brings together the best guitarists in the world to create an inspiring educational environment for the serious student of guitar.

For more information about Mr. Arnold check his website at http://www.brucearnold.com This website contains audio examples of Mr. Arnold's compositions and a workshop section with free downloadable music exercises.

Foreword

There is a direct correlation between a student's ability to identify pitches and their musicality. This ear training series presents a method with which I have had great success in improving my students' abilities to identify pitches, and provides a way to take one more step on the journey toward master musicianship. The course of study presented in this book assumes that the reader has intermediate to advanced knowledge of music.

Bruce Arnold

New York, New York

How to use this Book

Key note recognition refers to the ability to identify a pitch when heard against a key center. Each track of the separately available companion CD will play a chord progression which creates a cadence in a specific key and then plays the note C. From hearing this C you will try to identify which key you are in by the sound of the C note. My voice will then tell you what key was played so you can confirm whether you had the right answer. It is highly recommended that you work through all three levels of the Ear Training: One Note series before working with this book/CD, as you need to understand the concept of relating a pitch to a key center thoroughly. Please see the section at the end of this book for a complete list of titles and ISBN numbers or read pages 2-6.

Let's take a closer look at what exactly is transpiring as you listen to each track and how you should approach listening to this in your mind. Each track plays either a (ii-7 V7 IΔ7) or a (ii-7b5 V7b9 i-7) chord progression. You will hear this chord progression played 3 times, and then a repeated "one" chord. The aforementioned progression and the repeated "one" chord is there to ensure that your "ear" is placed into a key center. By hearing this progression your ear will be conditioned to hear in whatever key has been set up and therefore will relate any pitch it hears after the progression to that key. There are 24 tracks on the CD so all major and minor keys are represented.

Let's look even closer at what happens as you play a track on the CD. If you play track Two you will hear a (ii-7 V7 IΔ7) progression in the key of F major three times and then a repeated F major chord. By hearing the progression repeated over and over and then a reinforcing "one" chord your "ear" is firmly placed into the key of F major. The note C will then sound approximately 2-3 seconds later. Because your "ear" is in the key of F, any pitch you hear after this progression will be heard in relationship to this progression. Therefore the C should sound like the 5th of the key. C is the 5th of F major so you know that the chord progression you heard was a (ii-7 V7 IΔ7) progression in the key of F. (If you have trouble understanding this please read the background materials presented on pages 2-6).

There are many applications in the "real world" for this technique. Below are a couple of common examples:

1. If you walked into a room and a friend was playing a song or melody on an instrument, you could play one note on your instrument and instantly know what key he or she was playing in. Armed with that information you could start improvising in that key, or just playing along with them in the right key.

2. If someone played a chord progression that changed keys and you were asked to improvise over it, you would be able to listen to the notes you play and follow the key changes. For example: a chord progression might start in Ab, you would play a C, it would sound like the 3rd so you could improvise in Ab. Then you might come back to your C a few bars later and notice that it now sounded like the 6th; this would tell you that you have now modulated to Eb so you would start improvising in Eb.

A footnote: You will notice on the CD that the answers are sometime expressed in some rather remote and unusual keys. i.e. G# Major or D# Major. The reason for this is that I have found that it is easy to misunderstand someone when they say Bb or Eb because the sounds are so similar. In order to avoid confusion I have chosen key names that are less likely to be confused. It is perfectly all right to think of these sharp keys as flat keys if it is easier for you to internalize.

The following five pages are excerpted from the "Ear Training: One Note" books. If you have already worked through these books please skip to page 6. Doing ear training the "right" way is the only way you will develop a good ear. Please make sure that you understand the following pages before working on the Key Note Recognition CD.

Teaching Methods

There are many different approaches to developing pitch. Some of these methods are successful, some are not. First you must decide what kind of ear training will fit your needs. If you are a classical musician playing 20th century pieces that require you to play what may seem like random pitches with very few reference pitches to help you with intonation, you may find that developing perfect pitch is the most important goal for you. If you are a contemporary rock or jazz player playing improvised music you will find that developing relative pitch is far more important because it allows you to identify the keys that vamps, melodies and free improvisations are in, so you can respond with appropriate melodies or chords.

Commonly most courses of study for relative pitch concentrate on music dictation and singing melodies. Most colleges and high schools teach this way. But there are very real pitfalls to this method; most of these courses of study prepare a student to pass an exam but don't prepare a working musician for the skills they will need in a working situation. These courses fail to explain what to be listening for, and instead encourage the use of common tricks. These in turn lead to habits which stunt the student's progress. In some ways it is better if you've never done any ear training before starting the method presented here, because you won't have had a chance to develop the bad habits incorrect instruction can lead to.

Let's us talk about some of these teaching methods and why they simply do not work in the real world.

One of the most counterproductive assignments relative pitch ear training courses assign is to "learn all your intervals."

 A teacher sits down at a piano and starts playing different intervals and asks the class to identify which interval is being played. You may ask "What's so bad about that? All music is made up of different combinations of intervals so this should help me to identify pitch, right?"

Let's look closer. Let's say you have mastered this assignment; and any interval someone plays, you know what it is instantly. All right, great! Now you are on the band stand and the piano player is jamming along on a C major chord over and over and the bass player is playing a C note over and over. Most students with a little theory or practical experience know that playing a C chord over and over means the piece is in the key of C. Now your guitar player plays two notes which happen to be an E and a G. You instantly say "that's a minor 3rd that I hear. (The distance between E and G being 3 half steps which is commonly referred to as a minor 3rd) "All right" says the guitar player "well play it then," but now the real question has to be answered: what minor 3rd is it? If we examine the 12 pitches used in western music we find that there are 12 possible minor 3rd intervals that we could choose from. For example C to Eb, C# to E, D to F— all of these are minor 3rd intervals, and there are 12 possible minor 3rd intervals in all.

 How do you know which one it is?

The answer is you <u>don't</u> because you have only learned what a minor 3rd sounds like and not what the two pitches E and G sound like in the key. So something is missing here. You need to know more than what an interval sounds like; you need to know what notes sound like <u>in a key</u>. This is the first and major difference between the ear training contained in this book and that which is commonly taught in schools.

So, back to our example: if you knew what the 3rd and 5th of a key sounded like, you would have known which two notes the guitarist played. What the interval was between the two notes is of little importance when trying to identify pitch. The important thing to realize from this example is that **all 12 pitches have a unique sound against a key and this unique sound can be memorized.**

Let's go back to our teacher again and explore another problem that comes from teaching intervals. The teacher tells the student that it may help them to memorize intervals if they relate the intervals to songs they know. So the teacher suggests common melodies that they can use to help memorize these intervals, things like: a 4th is *Here Comes the Bride*, a 6th is *My Bonnie Lies over the Ocean*. So the student thinks "Wow this is great, now anytime I hear a 6th all I have to do is sing the first two notes of *My Bonnie Lies over the Ocean* and I'll know what notes are being played."

Once again let's look into this and explore two drawbacks of using common melodies to identify intervals:

1. The first two notes of *My Bonnie Lies over the Ocean* do comprise an interval of a 6th, but the 5th of the key up to the 3rd in the key is also a 6th.

Let's listen to this and see what happens when we play our "Bonnie 6th."

We're back on the bandstand playing a C chord vamp. The guitar player is playing the C chord with the bass playing a C, and the sax player plays a G (the fifth of the key) and then moves up to an E (the 3rd of the key) and you think "That's a sixth because I can hear that it is the beginning of *My Bonnie Lies over the Ocean*." Great! Now the sax player plays an Ab (the flat 6th of the key) and then moves up and plays an F (the 4th of the key). This is a sixth too, but can you easily hear *My Bonnie Lies over the Ocean* in this sound?

No.

This is because the first two notes of *My Bonnie Lies over the Ocean* are the 5th up to the 3rd of the key not the flat 6th to the 4th. So once again **the important thing is to learn what each note sounds like in a key, not what the distance is between notes.**

2. Let's say you're one of those students who has faithfully learned all your intervals and have developed the ability to grab a sound from any context and place an interval name on that sound by applying your memorized song to this interval.

All right— let's go back to our bandstand again and see how well it works as the band is jamming along.

Again the guitar player is playing the C chord with the bass playing a C and the sax player plays a G (the fifth of the key) and then moves up to an E (the 3rd of the key) the first thing that happens is you say to yourself "What is that sound I'm hearing," next you take that sound (the G up to E) and you run it through your mental rolodex of 11 basic intervals and the corresponding melodies that you have learned to identify these intervals. You come up with the correct answer and —Oops! The band is 2 bars past this point now and it's too late to use this information because it took you too long to calculate it. **Music moves by in time and the only relative pitch ear training that will help you is one that allows you the quickest identification of notes.**

Common Problems Associated with Ear Training

Let's also explore problems that creep up when students work on relative pitch ear training.

1. Our teacher plays a cadence I IV V I in the key of C which puts your "ear" into the key of C. Now the instructor plays an F. You immediately start singing up the scale from the root (C) to find the pitch the teacher is playing. You sing up to F and happily get the right answer. You get an "A+!"

But there's a problem here. Let's go back to our bandstand:

The guitar player is playing the C chord with the bass playing a C and the sax player plays an F (the fourth of the key) You now attempt to sing up the scale from the tonic that the bass and guitar are playing but whoa! Your guitarist has his double stack Marshall amplifier behind you with all knobs set on 11. You can't hear yourself sing up the scale to find out what pitch is being played.

So once again there's a problem. You can't rely on singing up to a note to identify it, you **just have to know by hearing the pitch what it's relationship is to a key.** I should also mention once again that by the time you have sung up the scale to find the pitch the band will have moved on, leaving you in the dust.

2. Here's another scenario: the teacher plays you a cadence I IV V I in the key of C which will put your "ear" into the key of C. Now the instructor plays an F#. You hear that this note exists outside of the key you have been set up to hear. (We say this note has *tension*.) When people encounter notes with these tensions, the common response is to resolve them, make them fit into the key (in this case, C) and then backtrack to name the note. F# commonly resolves up a half step to G so you now resolve the F# up in your mind to G which is the fifth. At that point you may be able to identify the G because you know the sound of the 5th of the key, or you may resolve the 5th down to the tonic or maybe you sing from the G note down the scale to C to get your answer. You may have finally gotten the correct answer but your method is flawed. First, you can't rely on resolution tendencies of notes because they don't always resolve the way you think they should when you place them in real music. Believe me, this resolution tendency will come back to haunt you later when you move on to two note ear training. And again, the time it takes for you to resolve this pitch in your mind is too long; you are in the dust once more.

So we are back to the fact that **You don't want to relate one pitch to another. You just want to know what each pitch sounds like in a key.**

Learning the Sound of Each Note

So how do we properly learn the sounds of all notes in a key? **Simply put, you need to memorize the sound of all 12 notes against a key center.** You can use no tricks. You must just listen to these notes over and over again until you start to internalize the unique sound of all 12 pitches against a key center. This is done two ways:

1. Listening to an Ear Training tape that gives you a cadence typically I IV V I in a key, then playing a note and trying to identify it. Remember that you must listen to each note with the proper mind set. First realize that the only way this ear training will work in real time is for it to become instantaneous. You must hear a note and just <u>know</u> what that note is. When you start don't be afraid to guess if you don't know the answer. It is much better to guess than to try to use some trick or relate it to something extraneous in your mind. Eventually you will memorize the sounds of each of these notes, but it takes time and repeated listening before this happens. You will memorize these sounds more quickly if you listen to your Ear Training CD 4 or 5 times a day for 15 minutes rather than doing a one hour session. This is because by listening to the CD at many different times throughout a day you will keep the sounds fresh in your short term memory and this will help to entrench the information in your long term memory.

2. Singing pitches against a recurring tonal center such as a repeating major chord; that is, the tonic of the key. Notice I did not say singing *melodies*, I said singing *pitches*. One of the first errors a student makes when sight singing is that he or she will memorize the melody that a group of notes creates rather than learning what these notes sound like in the key. The human ear/mind has this ability to memorize a melody while having no idea what the pitches are or how they relate to a key. For the beginning student it is crucial to concentrate more on the sounds of each pitch rather than to memorize a melody. This will help develop an affinity with the sound of that pitch. When you sing an exercise you shouldn't just blindly move from one pitch to another, you should try to hear the pitch in your head before you sing it. If you find you aren't hearing it at first, don't worry, this will come with practice. If you don't hear the pitch you need in your head, just play it on an instrument so you can hear it. Always try to hear the pitch in your head first though, because this will start to develop the sound in your mind. Eventually you should be able to wean yourself away from the instrument. Many times students will also try to identify a pitch by the way it resonates in the throat. This is not recommended; you just have to learn what the pitch sounds like in your mind's ear and then sing it. I recommend "A Fanatic's Guide to Ear Training and Sight Reading" ISBN #1890944750 for your singing exercises. The important thing is to have a recurring tonal center i.e. a repeating "one" chord sounding as you sing your pitches. The aforementioned book has a separately available CD for this purpose.

Ways to use the Key Note Recognition CD

The Ear Training CD works best if you use a CD player with shuffle play; this will prevent you from memorizing the order of the tracks. Many CD players, especially those found in computers, will also allow you to choose which tracks you would like to hear. This is particularly helpful if you have problems with certain keys. If your CD player also has "repeat" play you can use this to let the 24 tracks repeat themselves and shuffle their order. It is best to practice this CD in 10 to 20 minute increments several times throughout the day rather than in a marathon one hour session. By playing this CD often you keep these sounds and relationships in your short term memory which over time will move into your permanent memory.

WHAT NEXT?

Once you have mastered the Key Note Recognition book/CD it's time to move on to the two note ear training series of CDs. These books entitled Ear Training: Two Note can be found in the listing at the end of this book.

Names of the Keys found on the Separately available CD

Track 1. C Major
Track 2. F Major
Track 3. A# Major
Track 4. D# Major
Track 5. G# Major
Track 6. C# Major
Track 7. F# Major
Track 8. B Major
Track 9. E Major
Track 10. A Major
Track 11. D Major
Track 12. G Major
Track 13. C Minor
Track 14. F Minor
Track 15. A# Minor
Track 16. D# Minor
Track 17. G# Minor
Track 18. C# Minor
Track 19. F# Minor
Track 20. B Minor
Track 21. E Minor
Track 22. A Minor
Track 23. D Minor
Track 24. G Minor

Frequently Asked Questions

It is strongly recommended that you read through these questions that various students have submitted. Although this method of ear training is simple in concept, it is easy to do it incorrectly either through previous misleading musical training or just a misunderstanding on your part. If you don't proceed with this ear training with a good grasp of the concept, you will find that sooner or later you will hit a wall. The questions found here relate specifically to the following books: "Key Note Recognition," "Fanatic's Guide to Sight Singing and Ear Training," and "Ear Training: Two Note" book series

What level of music theory knowledge is needed to make significate improvement with your ear training method and what books to you recommend for improving my music theory knowledge?

There is definitely a level of music theory understanding needed in order to use the ear training skills taught in my books. As you move through the ear training series your grasp of music theory will have to be quicker and quicker. In order to excel in this ear training method you will need to know the note names of any degree of any key. You will need to know this in two ways: If you know the key center that you are hearing you will need to know what degree any note is within that key center. If you hear a note in a key center and you know the note you are hearing but not the key center you will have to know the degrees and notes that are in any given key center. To sum up: you will have to know how all 12 possible notes relate to all keys both as notes and as degrees of a key. If you feel the music theory part is slowing you down then I would recommend working through my music theory books.

I found your One Note Ear Training Series to be quite easy. Therefore I can't understand why I'm having so much trouble with the Key Note Recognition Book. Do you have any insights into why I'm having problems. I hear the C note after the progression and it doesn't sound like anything to me. Do you have any tips?

I think my first and most often repeated advice is to be patient. Most students find that Key Note Recognition is significantly harder than the One Note Ear Training Complete Series. There are a few reasons for this: You need to develop a better key retention ability because the key center is changing so you need to be able to lock into a key center right after hearing it and then sustain it in your mind until you hear the note. You can work on strengthening your key center retention by using the exercises in the Fanatic's Guide, pages 12 through 58. Try to get to the point where you can play a key center and then sing an entire page without hearing the key center again, yet still hear each note in the key center. This is extremely hard and it isn't recommended that you do this until you feel you can easily sing any exercise in the book with the CD's cadence and repeating one chord.

People also have a problem with Key Note Recognition because of the introduction of the minor keys. For many people this new sound confuses their ear and makes them perceive that all 12 notes against the key have somehow changed in their sound. It usually takes a few months of listening to these minor keys before you start to realize that the individual sounds are the same as in the major keys and that your ear was just confused by the overall minor sound.

When I hear notes against a minor key they sound different to me. For instance when I hear the 6th against a major key it sounds different from when I hear it against a minor key. Does this mean I need to learn a whole new set of sounds for minor.

When students are still weak in their recognition of one note they easily get confused when they hear certain notes against a minor key. In particular the major 3rd and the 6th are commonly confused. The major 3rd sound in a minor key is a sound that is very seldom heard in normal music so it will be quite strange for a while. Give yourself a few months of listening and you will see that this problem goes away.

Could you explain why Key Note Recognition is needed before working on the Ear Training: Two Note Series?

The Two Note series requires you to hold on to the sound of the cadence key while 2 notes are sounded and use that held sound to identify a possible new key center. Therefore you need to develop the ability to hear a sound against any key center and recognize how it is functioning in that key.

Could you give a couple of examples on how I would be able to use the ear training technique that Key Note Recognition is teaching me in a real life musical situation?

The ear training skills developed from Key Note Recognition will be some of the most useful in a real life playing situation. For instances if you are sitting in with a band and they start playing a tune that you don't know, you will be able to play one note and this will tell you what key they are playing in. Example: if the band is playing in G major and you play a C then the C will sound like the fourth. From your music theory you will know that C is the fourth of G major so you will know what key the band is playing in. This is extremely useful when soloing over changes that you don't know or are unsure as to what scale is required. If you just play a note and listen to its relationship to the key you will know what scale to play.

How long should I work on Key Note Recognition before moving on to the Ear Training: Two Note Series?

Because of the extreme difficulty found in the Two Note method you will need very solid preparation. You really want to have Key Note Recognition at or near 100% before moving on to the Ear Training: Two note series

Do you recommend working with the Fanatic's Guide to Sight Singing and Ear Training in conjunction with the Key Note Recognition book?

It is extremely important to work on singing exercises along with the One Note Ear Training and Key Note recognition. The Fanatic's Guide to Sight Singing and Ear Training was written with this in mind and would be a perfect companion for this training.

What books do you recommend using in conjunction with the Key Note Recognition book?

You definitely should be working out of Fanatic's Guide to Sight Singing and Ear Training. I would also continue to work with the One Note Ear Training CDs if you still feel weak. The music theory books are also good if you are still having problems identifying notes and degrees within a key.

How often should I listen to the Key Note Recognition CD?

I would recommend listening to the Key Note Recognition CD at least 5 or 6 times a day for 10 to 15 minutes.

A friend and I have been quizzing each other with our guitars using the method found on the Key Note Recognition CD. We have had some problems with doing this and find our recognition is much better with the CD then when we do it live with each other. Do you have any comments on why this is happening?

Students have reported both conditions: They can recognize better with the CD or better in a live situation. When students recognize more notes with the CD this is usually due in part to the fact that they have grown accustomed to the sound of the piano used on the CD and when they hear another instrument their ear gets confused. With all types of ear training (relative and perfect) it is common for people to infuse the sound of the instrument they hear with the notes they are trying to identify. As a person uses the ear training method more in everyday life they leave behind the instrument specific parts of their memory and just hear the quality of the note in a more abstract way.

I'm having a real difficulty figuring out how the C note relates to the key. It takes me forever to figure this out using music theory. Do you have any suggestions on how I can speed up the process?

I would recommend working with Music Theory Workbook Volume One to strengthen your music theory speed. You will also find that your theory knowledge will improve just from doing the Key Note Recognition exercises. Students often find that most of the music theory problems happen when they are in keys with which they are less knowledgable. I used to do an exercise while walking where I would pick a degree of a key and have to say what the note name was before I walked 2 or 3 steps. This exercise or something similar will help you speed up your response time.

I've been working with the Key Note CD for about five months(I'm a plodder) and finally have it at about (your recommended) 95% accuracy. I'm interested in your reaction to my plan. At this point I suppose that I could move on to the first 2 note volume, but my feeling is that without 100% mastery of this material (i.e. 100% accuracy, 100% of the time), I would be rushing things. Am I being too obsessive about this? I'm basing this on some of the ideas I have gleaned from Kenny Werner's book Effortless Mastery. It is his contention that we must practice to perfection and a state of effortless execution. I'm certainly not there yet with this stage, though I am close. What to do? Wait 'til the last 5% is in place consistently, or move on as recommended? What do you advise?

I understand your feelings about 100% accuracy, 100% of the time and I don't see any harm in waiting till you have a higher percentage than 95 but I also don't see a problem in moving on to two note ear training. This is based mostly on the fact that two note ear training makes you apply the skills you have developed so far in a slightly different way. Therefore many students find doing two note ear training actually helps them zero in on their previous weaknesses with one note. Because two note ear training is much harder for most students I certainly would never recommend moving on from one note until your one note and key note are at least at a 90% accuracy range. Some students also do one note, key note and two note ear training simultaneously until they have mastered one note and key note recognition,

When working with the Fanatic's Guide, is it an acceptable supplementary technique to sing the exercises while playing the changes to tunes and chord cycling exercises on my guitar? That seems like a powerful and valid technique to me, I'd just like to check as to whether there are any problems with it that haven't occurred to me. Thanks for your time. I'm really enjoying the work (ten months so far).

There can be a BIG problem with singing the exercises in Fanatic's Guide while playing the changes to tunes or chord cycling exercises, This is especially true if you attempt this before working on two note ear training. The reason for this is that two note ear training teaches you how to modulate, which of course many tunes do. If you want to do some supplemental singing I would get Single String Studies for Guitar Volume Two. Sing each page with a "one chord" drone like the tracks on the Fanatic's Guide CD. After you have been working with the two note ear training for a while let me know and I'll give you the next step in singing-which by the way is singing while playing the changes to tunes or chord cycling exercises (but you must do this in a particular way to receive the proper benefits).

How can I start to apply Key Note Recognition to real music?

I would take simple chord progressions and play one note on your instrument and see if you can identify the key the song is in. Keep in mind that certain chord progressions may sound like they are in one key one day and another key on another day. This is particularly true of some progressions found in rock and folk music where it constantly shifts between two keys because all the chords are closely related to 2 keys. Usually over time your ear will settle on one key but it may vacillate for a while.

Should I sing the C note when doing the Key Note Recognition to prepare me for 2 note ear training?

No, you shouldn't sing anything when doing Key Note Recognition.

Books Available From
Muse Eek Publishing Company

The Bruce Arnold series of instruction books for guitar are the result of 30 years of teaching. Mr. Arnold, who teaches at New York University and Princeton University has listened to the questions and problems of his students, and written over fifty books addressing the needs of the beginning to advanced student. Written in a direct, friendly and practical manner, each book is structured in such a way as to enable a student to understand, retain and apply musical information. In short, <u>these</u> <u>books</u> <u>teach</u>.

1st Steps for a Beginning Guitarist
Perfect Bound ISBN 1890944-93-9

1st Steps for a Beginning Guitarist is a comprehensive method for guitar students who have no prior musical training. Whether you are playing acoustic, electric or twelve-string guitar, this book will give you the information you need, and trouble shoot the various pitfalls that can hinder the self-taught musician. Includes pictures, videos and audio in the form of midifiles and mp3's.

Chord Workbook for Guitar Volume 1 (2nd edition)
Perfect Bound ISBN 1890944-50-5

<u>A consistent seller</u>, this book addresses the needs of the beginning through intermediate student. The beginning student will learn chords on the guitar, and a section is also included to help learn the basics of music theory. Progressions are provided to help the student apply these chords to common sequences. The more advanced student will find the reharmonization section to be an invaluable resource of harmonic choices. Information is given through musical notation as well as tablature.

Chord Workbook for Guitar Volume 2 (2nd edition)
Perfect Bound ISBN 1890944-51-3

This book is the Rosetta Stone of pop/jazz chords, and is geared to the intermediate to advanced student. These are the chords that any serious student bent on a musical career must know. Unlike other books which simply give examples of isolated chords, this unique book provides a comprehensive series of progressions and chord combinations which are immediately applicable to both composition and performance.

Music Theory Workbook for Guitar Series

The worlds most popular instrument, the guitar, is not taught in our public schools. In addition, it is one of the hardest on which to learn the basics of music. As a result, it is frequently difficult for the serious guitarist to get a firm foundation in theory.

Theory Workbook for Guitar Volume 1
Perfect Bound ISBN 1890944-52-1

This book provides real hands-on application of intervals and chords. A theory section written in concise and easy to understand language prepares the student for all exercises. Worksheets are given that quiz a student about intervals and chord construction using staff notation and guitar tablature. Answers are supplied in the back of the book enabling a student to work without a teacher.

Theory Workbook for Guitar Volume 2
Perfect Bound ISBN 1890944-53-X

This book provides real hands-on application for 22 different scale types. A theory section written in concise and easy to understand language prepares the student for all exercises. Worksheets are given that quiz a student about scale construction using staff notation and guitar tablature. Answers are supplied in the back of the book enabling a student to work without a teacher. Audio files are also available on the muse-eek.com website to facilitate practice and improvisation with all the scales presented.

Rhythm Book Series

These books are a breakthrough in music instruction, using the internet as a teaching tool! Audio files of all the exercises are easily downloaded from the internet.

Rhythm Primer
Perfect Bound ISBN 1890944-59-9

This 61 page book concentrates on all basic rhythms using four rhythmic levels. All examples use one pitch, allowing the student to focus completely on time and rhythm. All exercises can be downloaded from the internet to facilitate learning. See http://www.muse-eek.com for details

Rhythms Volume 1
Perfect Bound ISBN 1890944-55-6

This 120 page book concentrates on eighth note rhythms and is a thesaurus of rhythmic patterns. All examples use one pitch, allowing the student to focus completely on time and rhythm. All exercises can be downloaded from the internet to facilitate learning. See http://www.muse-eek.com for details.

Rhythms Volume 2
Perfect Bound ISBN 1890944-56-4

This volume concentrates on sixteenth note rhythms, and is a 108 page thesaurus of rhythmic patterns. All examples use one pitch, allowing the student to focus completely on time and rhythm. All exercises can be downloaded from the internet to facilitate learning. See http://www.muse-eek.com for details.

Rhythms Volume 3
Perfect Bound ISBN 1890944-57-2

This volume concentrates on thirty second note rhythms, and is a 102 page thesaurus of rhythmic patterns. All examples use one pitch, allowing the student to focus completely on time and rhythm. All exercises can be downloaded from the internet to facilitate learning. See http://www.muse-eek.com for details.

Odd Meters Volume 1
Perfect Bound ISBN 1890944-58-0

This book applies both eighth and sixteenth note rhythms to odd meter combinations. All examples use one pitch, allowing the student to focus completely on time and rhythm. Exercises can be downloaded from the internet to facilitate learning. This 100 page book is an essential sight reading tool. See http://www.muse-eek.com for details.

Contemporary Rhythms Volume 1
Perfect Bound ISBN 1890944-84-X

This volume concentrates on eight note rhythms and is a thesaurus of rhythmic patterns. Each exercise uses one pitch which allows the student to focus completely on time and rhythm. Exercises use modern innovations common to twentieth century notation, thereby familiarizing the student with the most sophisticated systems likely to be encountered in the course of a musical career. All exercises can be downloaded from the internet to facilitate learning. See http://www.muse-eek.com for details.

Contemporary Rhythms Volume 2
Perfect Bound ISBN 1890944-85-8

This volume concentrates on sixteenth note rhythms and is a thesaurus of rhythmic patterns. Each exercise uses one pitch which allows the student to focus completely on time and rhythm. Exercise use modern innovations common to twentieth century notation, thereby familiarizing the student with the most sophisticated systems likely to be encountered in the course of a musical career. All exercises can be downloaded from the internet to facilitate learning. See http://www.muse-eek.com for details.

Independence Volume 1
Perfect Bound ISBN 1890944-83-1

This 51 page book is designed for pianists, stick and touchstyle guitarists, percussionists and anyone who wishes to develop the rhythmic independence of their hands. This volume concentrates on quarter, eighth and sixteenth note rhythms and is a thesaurus of rhythmic patterns. The exercises in this book gradually incorporate more and more complex rhythmic patterns making it an excellent tool for both the beginning and the advanced student.

Other Guitar Study Aids

Right Hand Technique for Guitar Volume 1
Perfect Bound ISBN 1890944-54-8

Heres a breakthrough in music instruction, using the internet as a teaching tool! This book gives a concise method for developing right hand technique on the guitar, one of the most overlooked and under-addressed aspects of learning the instrument. The simplest, most basic movements are used to build fatigue-free technique. Exercises can be downloaded from the internet to facilitate learning. See http://www.muse-eek.com for details.

Single String Studies Volume One
Perfect Bound ISBN 1890944-62-9

This book is an excellent learning tool for both the beginner who has no experience reading music on the guitar, and the advanced student looking to improve their ledger line reading and general knowledge of each string of the guitar. Each exercise concentrates the students attention on one string at a time. This allows a familiarity to form between the written pitch and where it can be found on the guitar along with improving ones feel for jumping linearly across the fretboard. Exercises can be downloaded from the internet to facilitate learning. See http://www.muse-eek.com for details.

Single String Studies Volume Two
Perfect Bound ISBN 1890944-64-5

This book is a continuation of Volume One, but using non-diatonic notes. Volume Two helps the intermediate and advanced student improve their ledger line reading and general knowledge of each string of the guitar. Each exercise concentrates the students attention on one string at a time. This allows a familiarity to form between the written pitch and where it can be found on the guitar along with improving ones feel for jumping linearly across the fretboard. Exercises can be downloaded from the internet to facilitate learning. See http://www.muse-eek.com for details.

Single String Studies Volume One (Bass Clef)
Perfect Bound ISBN 1890944-63-7

This book is an excellent learning tool for both the beginner who has no experience reading music on the bass guitar, and the advanced student looking to improve their ledger line reading and general knowledge of each string of the bass. Each exercise concentrates a students attention of one string at a time. This allows a familiarity to form between the written pitch and where it can be found on the bass along with improving ones feel for jumping linearly across the fretboard. Exercises can be downloaded from the internet to facilitate learning. See http://www.muse-eek.com for details.

Single String Studies Volume Two (Bass Clef)
Perfect Bound ISBN 1890944-65-3

This book is a continuation of Volume One, but using non-diatonic notes. Volume Two helps the intermediate and advanced student improve their ledger line reading and general knowledge of each string of the bass. Each exercise concentrates the students attention on one string at a time. This allows a familiarity to form between the written pitch and where it can be found on the bass along with improving ones feel for jumping linearly across the fretboard. Exercises can be downloaded from the internet to facilitate learning. See http://www.muse-eek.com for details.

Guitar Clinic
Perfect Bound ISBN 1890944-86-6

Guitar Clinic contains techniques and exercises Mr. Arnold uses in the clinics and workshops he teaches around the U.S.. Much of the material in this book is culled from Mr. ArnoldÕs educational series, over thirty books in all. The student wishing to expand on his or her studies will find suggestions within the text as to which of Mr. Arnold's books will best serve their specific needs. Topics covered include: how to read music, sight reading, reading rhythms, music theory, chord and scale construction, modal sequencing, approach notes, reharmonization, bass and chord comping, and hexatonic scales.

The Essentials: Chord Charts, Scales, and Lead Patterns for the Guitar
Saddle Stitched (Stapled) ISBN 1-890944-94-7

This book is truly essential to the aspiring guitarist. It includes the most commonly played chords on the guitar in all keys, plus a bonus of the most commonly used scales and lead patterns. You can quickly learn all the chords, scales and lead patterns you need to know to play your favorite songs-and solo over them, too! The Essentials doesn't stop there, though. It also includes chord progressions to help you learn how to chord songs in folk, country, rock, blues and other popular styles. The books contain loads of easy to understand diagrams of chords, scales and lead patterns so you will be up and running in no time!

Sight Singing and Ear Training Series

The world is full of ear training and sight reading books, so why do we need more? This sight singing and ear training series uses a different method of teaching relative pitch sight singing and ear training. The success of this method has been remarkable. Along with a new method of ear training these books also use CDs and the internet as a teaching tool! Midifiles of many exercises are easily downloaded from the internet at www. muse-eek.com By combining interactive audio files with a new approach to ear training a student's progress is limited only by their willingness to practice!

A Fanatic's Guide to Ear Training and Sight Singing
Perfect Bound ISBN 1890944-75-0

This book and separately available CD present a method for developing good pitch recognition through sight singing. This method differs from the myriad of other sight singing books in that it develops the ability to identify and name all twelve pitches within a key center. Through this method a student gains the ability to identify sound based on it's relationship to a key and not the relationship of one note to another (i.e. interval training as commonly taught in many texts). All note groupings from one to six notes are presented giving the student a thesaurus of basic note combinations which develops sight singing and note recognition to a level unattainable before this Guide's existence.

Key Note Recognition
Perfect Bound ISBN 1890944-77-7

This book and separately available CD present a method for developing the ability to recognize the function of any note against a key. This method is a must for anyone who wishes to sound one note on an instrument or voice and instantly know what key a song is in. Through this method a student gains the ability to identify a sound based on its relationship to a key and not the relationship of one note to another (i.e. interval training as commonly taught in many texts). Key Center Recognition is a definite requirement before proceeding to two note ear training.

LINES Volume One: Sight Reading and Sight Singing Exercises
Perfect Bound ISBN 1890944-76-9

This book can be used for many applications. It is an excellent source for easy half note melodies that a beginner can use to learn how to read music or for sight singing slightly chromatic lines. An intermediate or advanced student will find exercises for multi-voice reading. These exercises can also be used for multi-voice ear training. The book has the added benefit in that all exercises can be heard by downloading the audio files for each example. See http://www.muse-eek.com for details.

LINES Volume Two: Sight Reading and Sight Singing Exercises
Perfect Bound ISBN 1594899-99-1

Recommended for those who have completed volume one, volume two introduces more complex harmonic material. This book can be used for many applications. It is an excellent source for easy quarter note melodies that a beginner can use to learn how to read music or for sight singing slightly chromatic lines. An intermediate or advanced student will find exercises for multi-voice reading. These exercises can also be used for multi-voice ear training. The book has the added benefit in that all exercises can be heard by downloading the audio files for each example. See http://www.muse-eek.com for details.

Ear Training ONE NOTE: Beginning Level
Perfect Bound ISBN 1890944-66-1

This Book and separately available audio CD present a new and exciting method for developing relative pitch ear training. It has been used with great success and is now finally available on CD. There are three levels available depending on the student's ability. This beginning level is recommended for students who have little or no music training.

Ear Training ONE NOTE: Intermediate Level
Perfect Bound ISBN 1890944-67-X

This book and separately available audio CD present a new and exciting method of developing relative pitch ear training. It has been used with great success and is now finally available on CD. This intermediate level is recommended for students who have had some music training but still find their skills need more development.

Ear Training ONE NOTE: Advanced Level
Perfect Bound ISBN 1890944-68-8

This book and separately available audio CD present a new and exciting method of developing relative pitch ear training. It has been used with great success and is now finally available on CD. There are three levels available depending on the student's ability. This advanced level is recommended for students who have worked with the intermediate level and now wish to perfect their skills.

Ear Training TWO NOTE: Beginning Level Volume One
Perfect Bound ISBN 1890944-69-6

This Book and separately available audio CD continues the method of developing relative pitch ear training as set forth in the "Ear Training, One Note" series. There are six volumes in the beginning level series. Through practice, the student eventually gains the ability to recognize the key and the names of any two notes played simultaneously. Volume One concentrates on 5ths. Prerequisite: a strong grasp of the One Note method.

Ear Training TWO NOTE: Beginning Level Volume Two
Perfect Bound ISBN 1890944-70-X

This Book and separately available audio CD continues the method of developing relative pitch ear training as set forth in the "Ear Training, One Note" series. There are six volumes in the beginning level series. Through practice, the student eventually gains the ability to recognize the key and the names of any two notes played simultaneously. Volume Two concentrates on 3rds. Prerequisite: a strong grasp of the One Note method.

Ear Training TWO NOTE: Beginning Level Volume Three
Perfect Bound ISBN 1890944-71-8

This Book and separately available audio CD continues the method of developing relative pitch ear training as set forth in the "Ear Training, One Note" series. There are six volumes in the beginning level series. Through practice, the student eventually gains the ability to recognize the key and the names of any two notes played simultaneously. Volume Three concentrates on 6ths. Prerequisite: a strong grasp of the One Note method.

Ear Training TWO NOTE: Beginning Level Volume Four
Perfect Bound ISBN 1890944-72-6

This Book and separately available audio CD continues the method of developing relative pitch ear training as set forth in the "Ear Training, One Note" series. There are six volumes in the beginning level series. Through practice, the student eventually gains the ability to recognize the key and the names of any two notes played simultaneously. Volume Four concentrates on 4ths. Prerequisite: a strong grasp of the One Note method.

Ear Training TWO NOTE: Beginning Level Volume Five
Perfect Bound ISBN 1890944-73-4

This Book and separately available audio CD continues the method of developing relative pitch ear training as set forth in the "Ear Training, One Note" series. There are six volumes in the beginning level series. Through practice, the student eventually gains the ability to recognize the key and the names of any two notes played simultaneously. Volume Five concentrates on 2nds. Prerequisite: a strong grasp of the One Note method.

Ear Training TWO NOTE: Beginning Level Volume Six
Perfect Bound ISBN 1890944-74-2

This Book and separately available audio CD continues the method of developing relative pitch ear training as set forth in the "Ear Training, One Note" series. There are six volumes in the beginning level series. Through practice, the student eventually gains the ability to recognize the key and the names of any two notes played simultaneously. Volume Six concentrates on 7ths. Prerequisite: a strong grasp of the One Note method.

Comping Styles Series

This series is built on the progressions found in Chord Workbook Volume One. Each book covers a specific style of music and presents exercises to help a guitarist, bassist or drummer master that style. Audio CDs are also available so a student can play along with each example and really get "into the groove."

Comping Styles for the Guitar Volume Two FUNK
Perfect Bound ISBN 1890944-60-2

This volume teaches a student how to play guitar or piano in a funk style. 36 Progressions are presented: 12 keys of a Major and Minor Blues plus 12 keys of Rhythm Changes A different groove is presented for each exercise giving the student a wide range of funk rhythms to master. A separately available audio CD is also included so a student can play along with each example and really get "into the groove." The audio CD contains "trio" versions of each exercise with Guitar, Bass and Drums.

Comping Styles for the Bass Volume Two FUNK
Perfect Bound ISBN 1890944-61-0

This volume teaches a student how to play bass in a funk style. 36 Progressions are presented: 12 keys of a Major and Minor Blues plus 12 keys of Rhythm Changes A different groove is presented for each exercise giving the student a wide range of funk rhythms to master. A separately available audio CD is also included so a student can play along with each example and really get "into the groove." The audio CD contains "trio" versions of each exercise with Guitar, Bass and Drums.

Jazz and Blues Bass Line
Perfect Bound ISBN 1890944-16-5

This book covers the basics of bass line construction. A theoretical guide to building bass lines is presented along with 36 chord progressions utilizing the twelve keys of a Major and Minor Blues, plus twelve keys of Rhythm Changes. A reharmonization section is also provided which demonstrates how to reharmonize a chord progression on the spot. A separately available audio CD allows a student can play along with each example.

Time Series

The Doing Time series presents a method for contacting, developing and relying on your internal time sense: This series is an excellent resource for any musician who is serious about developing strong internal sense of time. This is particularly useful in any kind of music where the rhythms and time signatures may be very complex or free, and there is no conductor.

THE BIG METRONOME
Spiral Bound ISBN 1-890944-37-8   Perfect Bound ISBN 1890944-82-3

The Big Metronome is designed to help you develop a better internal sense of time. This is accomplished by requiring you to "feel time" rather than having you rely on the steady click of a metronome. The idea is to slowly wean yourself away from an external device and rely on your internal/natural sense of time. The exercises presented work in conjunction with the three separately available CDs. CD 1 presents the first 13 settings from a traditional metronome 40-66; the second CD contains metronome markings 69-116, and the third CD contains metronome markings 120-208. The first CD gives you a 2 bar count off and a click every measure, the second CD gives you a 2 bar count off and a click every 2 measures, the 3rd CD gives you a 2 bar count off and a click every 4 measures. By presenting all common metronome markings a student can use these 3 CDs as a replacement for a traditional metronome.

Doing Time with the Blues Volume One
Perfect Bound ISBN 1890944-78-5

The book and separately available CD presents a method for gaining an internal sense of time thereby eliminating dependence on a metronome. The book presents the basic concept for developing good time and also includes exercises that can be practiced with the CD. The CD provides eight 8 minute tracks at different tempos in which the time is delineated every 2 bars, and with an extra hit every 12 bars to outline the blues form. The student may then use the exercises presented in the book to gain control of their execution or improvise to gain control of their ideas using this bare minimum of time delineation.

Doing Time with the Blues Volume Two
Perfect Bound ISBN 1890944-79-3

This is the 2nd volume of a four volume series which presents a method for developing a musicians internal sense of time, thereby eliminating dependence on a metronome. This 2nd volume presents different exercises which further the development of this time sense. This 2nd volume begins to test even a professional level players ability. The separately available CD provides eight 8 minute tracks at different tempos in which the time is delineated every 4 bars with an extra hit every 12 bars to outline the blues form. New exercises are also included that can be practiced with the CD. This series is an excellent resource for any musician who is serious about developing an internal sense of time.

Doing Time with 32 Bars Volume One
Perfect Bound ISBN 1890944-80-7

The book and separately available CD presents a method for gaining an internal sense of time thereby eliminating dependence on a metronome. The book presents the basic concept for developing good time and also includes exercises that can be practiced with the CD. The CD provides eight 8 minute tracks at different tempos in which the time is delineated every 2 bars, with an extra hit every 32 to outline the 32 bar form. The student may then use the exercises presented in the book to gain control of their execution or improvise to gain control of their ideas using this bare minimum of time delineation.

Doing Time with 32 Bars Volume Two
Perfect Bound ISBN 1890944-81-5

This is the 2nd volume of a four volume series which presents a method for developing a musicians internal sense of time, thereby eliminating dependence on a metronome.. This 2nd volume presents different exercises which further the development of this time sense. This 2nd volume begins to test even a professional level players ability. The separately available CD provides eight 8 minute tracks at different tempos in which the time is delineated every 4 bars with an extra hit every 32 bars to outline the 32 bar form. New exercises are also included that can be practiced with the CD. This series is an excellent resource for any musician who is serious about developing an internal sense of time.

Time Transformation
Perfect Bound ISBN 1594899-930-4

"Time Transformation" is designed to take the application of odd meters to another level of mastery. Etudes are presented in 12 keys using the time signatures of 3/4, 4/4, 5/4, 6/4 and 7/4. There are a total of 60 highly syncopated studies that are presented using various combinations of eighth note and sixteenth note rhythms. Book also includes downloadable "vamps" that can be used in various ways with each étude.

Other Workbooks

Music Theory Workbook for All Instruments, Volume 1: Interval and Chord Construction
Perfect Bound ISBN 1890944-46-7

This book provides real hands-on application of intervals and chords. A theory section written in concise and easy to understand language prepares the student for all exercises. Worksheets are given that quiz a student about intervals and chord construction using staff notation. Answers are supplied in the back of the book enabling a student to work without a teacher.

Jazz Piano Vocabulary by Roberta Piket, Volume 1: The Major Scale
Perfect Bound ISBN 1594899-51-7

This is the 1st volume in a series designed to help the student of jazz piano learn and apply jazz scales by mastering each scale and its uses in improvisation. Each book focuses on a different scale, illustrating the scale in all twelve keys with complete fingerings. Also provided are chords and left hand voicings to match, exercises and études to apply the material to improvising, ideas for further study and listening, and detailed suggestions on how to prace the material. Volume 1 also includes a detailed primer in note reading, basic theory, and rhythmic notation.

Jazz Piano Vocabulary by Roberta Piket, Volume 2: The Dorian Mode
Perfect Bound ISBN 1890944-98-X

The 2nd volume in the series, this book focuses on the Dorian scale and applies it to improvising on minor seventh chords. The Dorian scale is presented in all twelve keys with complete fingerings. The book also contains left hand voicings, exercises, many examples, an étude to help apply the material, ideas for further study, an extended discography, and detailed instruction and practice tips.

Jazz Piano Vocabulary by Roberta Piket, Volume 3: The Phrygian Mode
Perfect Bound ISBN 1594899-54-1

For students who have covered the basics in Volume 1,2 and 5, this book focuses in the Phrygian and Spanish Phrygian scales. It discusess "modern" jazz chords such as the "Phrygian" chord (susb9). The scale is presented in all 12 keys with fingerings. It also provides a detailed treatise on a modal approach to chord voicings, practice tips and a Phrygian étude.

Jazz Piano Vocabulary by Roberta Piket, Volume 4: The Lydian Mode
Perfect Bound ISBN 1594899-56-8

Volume 4 features the Lydian scale in all twelve keys; two octaves up and down with complete piano fingerings. Chords are presented with left hand voicings that work with the scale (along with fingerings) Also included are exercises to develop the concept of melodic phrasing in improvisation, examples of the use of the Lydian scale in the jazz repertoire, and detailed instructions on how to practice the material. Added feature: author can be contacted online if questions arise.

Jazz Piano Vocabulary by Roberta Piket, Volume 5: The Mixolydian Mode
Perfect Bound ISBN 1594899-58-4

This book focuses on the Mixolydian scale and applies it to improvising on dominant seventh and dominant seventh sus chords. The scale is presented in all twelve keys with fingerings. The book also contains an introduction to approach notes, an explanation and étude on twelve bar blues form, left hand voicings, exercises, melodic examples, instruction and practice tips.

Guitar Method Series

This series of books distills several of our previous publications into a method currently in use at New York University for the Summer Guitar Intensive Program. Content is geared towards any musician that is looking to expand their understanding of typical musical concepts but also covers many musically uncharted territories. Material concentrates on essential information the student must master in order to become a professional guitarist in the heavily competitive New York City music scene. This series of books starts with the most basic beginning guitar information and takes the reader to the most advanced musical concepts.

New York Guitar Method Primer Book 1
Perfect Bound ISBN 159489-912-6

This book provides students with an excellent foundation in theory, ear training, chord and scale comprehension on the guitar. It is a prerequisite for entering New York University's Summer Guitar Intensive Program and provides students studying independently with the tools they will need to successfully move on to Primer Book 2.

New York Guitar Method Primer Book 2
Perfect Bound ISBN 159489-916-9

This book provides students with an excellent foundation in theory, ear training, chord and scale comprehension on the guitar. It is a prerequisite for entering New York University's Summer Guitar Intensive Program and provides students studying independently with the tools they will need to successfully move on to New York Guitar Method Book 1. "New York Guitar Method Primer Ensemble Book Two" is the companion book for "New York Guitar Method Primer Book Two." This book contains music examples of the information covered in this book so that a student can apply the information through memorization and sight reading.

New York Guitar Method Primer Ensemble Book 2
Perfect Bound ISBN 159489-914-2

This book is a prerequisite for entering New York University's Summer Guitar Intensive Program and provides students studying independently with the tools they will need to successfully move on to Volume 1. Our Ensemble Method presents a breakthrough approach for teaching guitarist how to sightread. Each chapter has eighth note, sixteenth note, single string, lines, and chord exercises. The book also includes modal jazz vamps and solos and is an excellent resource for lab/ensemble studies as it contains 3 and 4-part reading examples.

New York Guitar Method Volume 1
Perfect Bound ISBN 159489-900-2

This book contains 22 scales and their theory which are covered in great detail. Multiple types of chord voicings along with an in-Depth coverage of articulations. The application of scales through modal sequences is also explained. The following musical concepts are covered: Finding the Right Scale for Any Chord, Finding the Natural Scale Sound, Thinking the Way You Hear, Two to Eleven Note Scale Possibilities along with a list of 2,048 Scale Possibilities which contain the root. Slash Chords, Regular Chords and Slash Chords, Slash Chord Possibilities, Reharmonization Theory, Adding Tensions.
"New York Guitar Method Ensemble Book One" is the companion book for "New York Guitar Method Volume One." This book contains music examples of the information covered in this book so that a student can apply the information through memorization and sight reading.

New York Guitar Method Ensemble Book 1
Perfect Bound ISBN 159489-906-1

Volume One focuses on reading jazz solos that demonstrate the many uses of scales as discussed in the accompanying New York Guitar Method Volume 1. The book also includes jazz and classical reading études and is an excellent resource for lab/ensemble studies as it contains 3 and 4-part reading examples.

New York Guitar Method Volume 2
Perfect Bound ISBN 159489-902-9

This is the second book in our series currently in use at New York University for the Summer Guitar Intensive Program. A continuation of Volume 1, Volume 2 focuses on approach notes and discusses how to apply approaches to jazz lines in order to create the signature sounding lines of bebop through the contemporary sounding lines of the modern masters. "New York Guitar Method Ensemble Book Two" is the companion book for "New York Guitar Method Volume Two." This book contains music examples of the information covered in this book so that a student can apply the information through memorization and sight reading.

New York Guitar Method Ensemble Book 2
Perfect Bound ISBN 159489-908-8
   Volume Two focuses on reading jazz solos that demonstrate the many uses of approach notes as discussed in the accompanying New York Guitar Method Volume 2. The book also includes jazz and classical reading études and is an excellent resource for lab/ensemble studies as it contains 3 and 4-part reading examples.

Set Theory Method

   This series of books explores the relationships of post tonal theory to contemporary improvisation. It is meant to bridge the gap between jazz theory and contemporary set theory.

Sonic Resource Guide
Perfect Bound ISBN 159489-934-7

   "Set Theory for Improvisation" examines the use and organization of pitch class sets for improvisation and composition. Two through twelve note pitch class sets are explored and their application to the harmony and melody shown through multiple examples. The companion series "Set Theory for Improvisation Ensemble" is recommended as both a overall musical development tool and as a sight reading gold mine. For all instruments.

Set Theory for Improvisation Ensemble Method

   The ensemble method gives examples of applying post tonal theory to contemporary improvisation in the form of études. Each étude explores the melodic possibilities using various combinations of note groupings, rhythms, metric level, melodic range and density. There are 12 études in each book, one in each key which can be played over a variety of chords. These études range from highly diatonic to non-diatonic examples depending on the organization of the material. For all instruments.

Set Theory for Improvisation Ensemble Method: Hexatonic 027 027
Perfect Bound ISBN 159489-921-5

Set Theory for Improvisation Ensemble Method: Hexatonic 027 016
Perfect Bound ISBN 159489-923-1

Set Theory for Improvisation Ensemble Method: Hexatonic 027 026
Perfect Bound ISBN 159489-925-8

E-Books

The Bruce Arnold series of instructional E-books is for the student who wishes to target specific areas of study that are of particular interest. Many of these books are excerpted from other larger texts. The excerpted source is listed for each book. These books are available on-line at www.muse-eek.com as well as at many e-tailers throughout the internet. These books can also be purchased in the traditional book binding format. (See the ISBN number for proper format)

Chord Velocity: Volume One, Learning to switch between chords quickly
E-book ISBN 1-890944-88-2

The first hurdle a beginning guitarist encounters is difficulty in switching between chords quickly enough to make a chord progression sound like music. This book provides exercises that help a student gradually increase the speed with which they change chords. Special free audio files are also available on the muse-eek.com website to make practice more productive and fun. Within a few weeks, remarkable improvement can be achieved using this method. This book is excerpted from "1st Steps for a Beginning Guitarist Volume One."

Guitar Technique: Volume One, Learning the basics to fast, clean, accurate and fluid performance skills.
E-book ISBN 1-890944-91-2

This book is for both the beginning guitarist or the more experienced guitarist who wishes to improve their technique. All aspects of the physical act of playing the guitar are covered, from how to hold a guitar to the specific way each hand is involved in the playing process. Pictures and videos are provided to help clarify each technique. These pictures and videos are either contained in the book or can be downloaded at www. muse-eek.com This book is excerpted from "1st Steps for a Beginning Guitarist Volume One."

Accompaniment: Volume One, Learning to Play Bass and Chords Simultaneously
E-book ISBN 1-890944-87-4

The techniques found within this book are an excellent resource for creating and understanding how to play bass and chords simultaneously in a jazz or blues style. Special attention is paid to understanding how this technique is created, thereby enabling the student to recreate this style with other pieces of music. This book is excerpted from the book "Guitar Clinic."

Beginning Rhythm Studies: Volume One, Learning the basics of reading rhythm and playing in time.
E-book ISBN 1-890944-89-0

This book covers the basics for anyone wishing to understand or improve their rhythmic abilities. Simple language is used to show the student how to read and play rhythm. Exercises are presented which can accelerate the learning process. Audio examples in the form of midifiles are available on the muse-eek. com website to facilitate learning the correct rhythm in time. This book is excerpted from the book "Rhythm Primer."

This log is for keeping track of keys that are giving you a problem. You can use this to track which keys need more work or the common mistakes you make.

Key:_____   Answer Given_____

Key:_____   Answer Given_____

Key:_____   Answer Given_____

Key:_____   Answer Given_____

Key:_____   Answer Given_____

Key:_____   Answer Given_____

Key:_____   Answer Given_____

Key:_____   Answer Given_____

Key:_____   Answer Given_____

Key:_____   Answer Given_____

Key:_____   Answer Given_____

Key:_____   Answer Given_____

Key:_____   Answer Given_____

Key:_____   Answer Given_____

Key:_____   Answer Given_____

Key:_____   Answer Given_____

Key:_____   Answer Given_____

Key:_____   Answer Given_____

Key:_____   Answer Given_____

Key:_____   Answer Given_____

Key:_____   Answer Given_____

Key:_____   Answer Given_____

Key:_____   Answer Given_____

Key:_____   Answer Given_____

Key:_____   Answer Given_____

Key:_____   Answer Given_____

Key:_____   Answer Given_____

Key:_____   Answer Given_____

Key:_____   Answer Given_____

Key:_____   Answer Given_____

Key:_____   Answer Given_____

Key:_____   Answer Given_____

Key:_____   Answer Given_____

Key:_____   Answer Given_____

Key:_____   Answer Given_____

Key:_____   Answer Given_____

Key:_____   Answer Given_____

Key:_____   Answer Given_____

Key:_____   Answer Given_____

Key:_____   Answer Given_____

Key:_____   Answer Given_____

Key:_____   Answer Given_____

Key:_____   Answer Given_____

Key:_____   Answer Given_____

Key:_____   Answer Given_____

Key:_____   Answer Given_____

Key:_____   Answer Given_____

Key:_____   Answer Given_____

Key:_____   Answer Given_____

Key:_____   Answer Given_____

Key:_____   Answer Given_____

Key:_____   Answer Given_____

Key:_____   Answer Given_____

Key:_____   Answer Given_____

Key:_____   Answer Given_____

Key:_____   Answer Given_____

Key:_____   Answer Given_____

Key:_____   Answer Given_____

Key:_____   Answer Given_____

Key:_____   Answer Given_____

Key:_____   Answer Given_____

Key:_____   Answer Given_____

Key:_____   Answer Given_____

Key:_____   Answer Given_____

Key:_____	Answer Given_____
Key:_____	Answer Given_____
Key:_____	Answer Given_____
Key:_____	Answer Given_____
Key:_____	Answer Given_____
Key:_____	Answer Given_____
Key:_____	Answer Given_____
Key:_____	Answer Given_____
Key:_____	Answer Given_____
Key:_____	Answer Given_____
Key:_____	Answer Given_____
Key:_____	Answer Given_____
Key:_____	Answer Given_____
Key:_____	Answer Given_____
Key:_____	Answer Given_____
Key:_____	Answer Given_____
Key:_____	Answer Given_____
Key:_____	Answer Given_____
Key:_____	Answer Given_____
Key:_____	Answer Given_____
Key:_____	Answer Given_____
Key:_____	Answer Given_____
Key:_____	Answer Given_____
Key:_____	Answer Given_____
Key:_____	Answer Given_____
Key:_____	Answer Given_____
Key:_____	Answer Given_____
Key:_____	Answer Given_____
Key:_____	Answer Given_____
Key:_____	Answer Given_____
Key:_____	Answer Given_____
Key:_____	Answer Given_____
Key:_____	Answer Given_____

Key:_____ Answer Given_____

Key:_____ Answer Given_____

Key:_____ Answer Given_____

Key:_____ Answer Given_____

Key:_____ Answer Given_____

Key:_____ Answer Given_____

Key:_____ Answer Given_____

Key:_____ Answer Given_____

Key:_____ Answer Given_____

Key:_____ Answer Given_____

Key:_____ Answer Given_____

Key:_____ Answer Given_____

Key:_____ Answer Given_____

Key:_____ Answer Given_____

Key:_____ Answer Given_____

Key:_____ Answer Given_____

Key:_____ Answer Given_____

Key:_____ Answer Given_____

Key:_____ Answer Given_____

Key:_____ Answer Given_____

Key:_____ Answer Given_____

Key:_____ Answer Given_____

Key:_____ Answer Given_____

Key:_____ Answer Given_____

Key:_____ Answer Given_____

Key:_____ Answer Given_____

Key:_____ Answer Given_____

Key:_____ Answer Given_____

Key:_____ Answer Given_____

Key:_____ Answer Given_____

Key:_____ Answer Given_____

Key:_____ Answer Given_____

Key:_____ Answer Given_____

Key:_____ Answer Given_____

Key:_____	Answer Given_____
Key:_____	Answer Given_____
Key:_____	Answer Given_____
Key:_____	Answer Given_____
Key:_____	Answer Given_____
Key:_____	Answer Given_____
Key:_____	Answer Given_____
Key:_____	Answer Given_____
Key:_____	Answer Given_____
Key:_____	Answer Given_____
Key:_____	Answer Given_____
Key:_____	Answer Given_____
Key:_____	Answer Given_____
Key:_____	Answer Given_____
Key:_____	Answer Given_____
Key:_____	Answer Given_____
Key:_____	Answer Given_____
Key:_____	Answer Given_____
Key:_____	Answer Given_____
Key:_____	Answer Given_____
Key:_____	Answer Given_____
Key:_____	Answer Given_____
Key:_____	Answer Given_____
Key:_____	Answer Given_____
Key:_____	Answer Given_____
Key:_____	Answer Given_____
Key:_____	Answer Given_____
Key:_____	Answer Given_____
Key:_____	Answer Given_____
Key:_____	Answer Given_____
Key:_____	Answer Given_____
Key:_____	Answer Given_____
Key:_____	Answer Given_____

Key:_____   Answer Given_____

Key:_____   Answer Given_____

Key:_____   Answer Given_____

Key:_____   Answer Given_____

Key:_____   Answer Given_____

Key:_____   Answer Given_____

Key:_____   Answer Given_____

Key:_____   Answer Given_____

Key:_____   Answer Given_____

Key:_____   Answer Given_____

Key:_____   Answer Given_____

Key:_____   Answer Given_____

Key:_____   Answer Given_____

Key:_____   Answer Given_____

Key:_____   Answer Given_____

Key:_____   Answer Given_____

Key:_____   Answer Given_____

Key:_____   Answer Given_____

Key:_____   Answer Given_____

Key:_____   Answer Given_____

Key:_____   Answer Given_____

Key:_____   Answer Given_____

Key:_____   Answer Given_____

Kcy:_____   Answcr Givcn_____

Key:_____   Answer Given_____

Key:_____   Answer Given_____

Key:_____   Answer Given_____

Key:_____   Answer Given_____

Key:_____   Answer Given_____

Key:_____   Answer Given_____

Key:_____   Answer Given_____

Key:_____   Answer Given_____

Key:_____	Answer Given_____
Key:_____	Answer Given_____
Key:_____	Answer Given_____
Key:_____	Answer Given_____
Key:_____	Answer Given_____
Key:_____	Answer Given_____
Key:_____	Answer Given_____
Key:_____	Answer Given_____
Key:_____	Answer Given_____
Key:_____	Answer Given_____
Key:_____	Answer Given_____
Key:_____	Answer Given_____
Key:_____	Answer Given_____
Key:_____	Answer Given_____
Key:_____	Answer Given_____
Key:_____	Answer Given_____
Key:_____	Answer Given_____
Key:_____	Answer Given_____
Key:_____	Answer Given_____
Key:_____	Answer Given_____
Key:_____	Answer Given_____
Key:_____	Answer Given_____
Key:_____	Answer Given_____
Key:_____	Answer Given_____
Key:_____	Answer Given_____
Key:_____	Answer Given_____
Key:_____	Answer Given_____
Key:_____	Answer Given_____
Key:_____	Answer Given_____
Key:_____	Answer Given_____
Key:_____	Answer Given_____
Key:_____	Answer Given_____
Key:_____	Answer Given_____
Key:_____	Answer Given_____

Key:_____	Answer Given_____
Key:_____	Answer Given_____
Key:_____	Answer Given_____
Key:_____	Answer Given_____
Key:_____	Answer Given_____
Key:_____	Answer Given_____
Key:_____	Answer Given_____
Key:_____	Answer Given_____
Key:_____	Answer Given_____
Key:_____	Answer Given_____
Key:_____	Answer Given_____
Key:_____	Answer Given_____
Key:_____	Answer Given_____
Key:_____	Answer Given_____
Key:_____	Answer Given_____
Key:_____	Answer Given_____
Key:_____	Answer Given_____
Key:_____	Answer Given_____
Key:_____	Answer Given_____
Key:_____	Answer Given_____
Key:_____	Answer Given_____
Key:_____	Answer Given_____
Key:_____	Answer Given_____
Key:_____	Answer Given_____
Kcy:_____	Answer Given_____
Key:_____	Answer Given_____
Key:_____	Answer Given_____
Key:_____	Answer Given_____
Key:_____	Answer Given_____
Key:_____	Answer Given_____
Key:_____	Answer Given_____
Key:_____	Answer Given_____
Key:_____	Answer Given_____
Key:_____	Answer Given_____

Key:_____	Answer Given_____
Key:_____	Answer Given_____
Key:_____	Answer Given_____
Key:_____	Answer Given_____
Key:_____	Answer Given_____
Key:_____	Answer Given_____
Key:_____	Answer Given_____
Key:_____	Answer Given_____
Key:_____	Answer Given_____
Key:_____	Answer Given_____
Key:_____	Answer Given_____
Key:_____	Answer Given_____
Key:_____	Answer Given_____
Key:_____	Answer Given_____
Key:_____	Answer Given_____
Key:_____	Answer Given_____
Key:_____	Answer Given_____
Key:_____	Answer Given_____
Key:_____	Answer Given_____
Key:_____	Answer Given_____
Key:_____	Answer Given_____
Key:_____	Answer Given_____
Key:_____	Answer Given_____
Key:_____	Answer Given_____
Key:_____	Answer Given_____
Key:_____	Answer Given_____
Key:_____	Answer Given_____
Key:_____	Answer Given_____
Key:_____	Answer Given_____
Key:_____	Answer Given_____
Key:_____	Answer Given_____
Key:_____	Answer Given_____
Key:_____	Answer Given_____
Key:_____	Answer Given_____

Key:_____   Answer Given_____

Key:_____   Answer Given_____

Key:_____   Answer Given_____

Key:_____   Answer Given_____

Key:_____   Answer Given_____

Key:_____   Answer Given_____

Key:_____   Answer Given_____

Key:_____   Answer Given_____

Key:_____   Answer Given_____

Key:_____   Answer Given_____

Key:_____   Answer Given_____

Key:_____   Answer Given_____

Key:_____   Answer Given_____

Key:_____   Answer Given_____

Key:_____   Answer Given_____

Key:_____   Answer Given_____

Key:_____   Answer Given_____

Key:_____   Answer Given_____

Key:_____   Answer Given_____

Key:_____   Answer Given_____

Key:_____   Answer Given_____

Key:_____   Answer Given_____

Key:_____   Answer Given_____

Key:_____   Answer Given_____

Key:_____   Answer Given_____

Key:_____   Answer Given_____

Key:_____   Answer Given_____

Key:_____   Answer Given_____

Key:_____   Answer Given_____

Key:_____   Answer Given_____

Key:_____   Answer Given_____

Key:_____   Answer Given_____

Key:_____   Answer Given_____

Key:_____   Answer Given_____

Key:_____   Answer Given_____

Key:_____   Answer Given_____

Key:_____   Answer Given_____

Key:_____   Answer Given_____

Key:_____	Answer Given_____
Key:_____	Answer Given_____
Key:_____	Answer Given_____
Key:_____	Answer Given_____
Key:_____	Answer Given_____
Key:_____	Answer Given_____
Key:_____	Answer Given_____
Key:_____	Answer Given_____
Key:_____	Answer Given_____
Key:_____	Answer Given_____
Key:_____	Answer Given_____
Key:_____	Answer Given_____
Key:_____	Answer Given_____
Key:_____	Answer Given_____
Key:_____	Answer Given_____
Key:_____	Answer Given_____
Key:_____	Answer Given_____
Key:_____	Answer Given_____
Key:_____	Answer Given_____
Key:_____	Answer Given_____
Key:_____	Answer Given_____
Key:_____	Answer Given_____
Key:_____	Answer Given_____
Key:_____	Answer Given_____
Key:_____	Answer Given_____
Key:_____	Answer Given_____
Key:_____	Answer Given_____
Key:_____	Answer Given_____
Key:_____	Answer Given_____
Key:_____	Answer Given_____
Key:_____	Answer Given_____
Key:_____	Answer Given_____
Key:_____	Answer Given_____
Key:_____	Answer Given_____
Key:_____	Answer Given_____
Key:_____	Answer Given_____

Key:_____   Answer Given_____

Key:_____   Answer Given_____

Key:_____   Answer Given_____

Key:_____   Answer Given_____

Key:_____   Answer Given_____

Key:_____   Answer Given_____

Key:_____   Answer Given_____

Key:_____   Answer Given_____

Key:_____   Answer Given_____

Key:_____   Answer Given_____

Key:_____   Answer Given_____

Key:_____   Answer Given_____

Key:_____   Answer Given_____

Key:_____   Answer Given_____

Key:_____   Answer Given_____

Key:_____   Answer Given_____

Key:_____   Answer Given_____

Key:_____   Answer Given_____

Key:_____   Answer Given_____

Key:_____   Answer Given_____

Key:_____   Answer Given_____

Key:_____   Answer Given_____

Key:_____   Answer Given_____

Key:_____   Answer Given_____

Key:_____   Answer Given_____

Key:_____   Answer Given_____

Key:_____   Answer Given_____

Key:_____   Answer Given_____

Key:_____   Answer Given_____

Key:_____   Answer Given_____

Key:_____   Answer Given_____

Key:_____   Answer Given_____

Key:_____   Answer Given_____

Key:_____	Answer Given_____
Key:_____	Answer Given_____
Key:_____	Answer Given_____
Key:_____	Answer Given_____
Key:_____	Answer Given_____
Key:_____	Answer Given_____
Key:_____	Answer Given_____
Key:_____	Answer Given_____
Key:_____	Answer Given_____
Key:_____	Answer Given_____
Key:_____	Answer Given_____
Key:_____	Answer Given_____
Key:_____	Answer Given_____
Key:_____	Answer Given_____
Key:_____	Answer Given_____
Key:_____	Answer Given_____
Key:_____	Answer Given_____
Key:_____	Answer Given_____
Key:_____	Answer Given_____
Key:_____	Answer Given_____
Key:_____	Answer Given_____
Key:_____	Answer Given_____
Key:_____	Answer Given_____
Key:_____	Answer Given_____
Key:_____	Answer Given_____
Key:_____	Answer Given_____
Key:_____	Answer Given_____
Key:_____	Answer Given_____
Key:_____	Answer Given_____
Key:_____	Answer Given_____
Key:_____	Answer Given_____
Key:_____	Answer Given_____
Key:_____	Answer Given_____
Key:_____	Answer Given_____

Key:_____   Answer Given_____
Key:_____   Answer Given_____
Key:_____   Answer Given_____
Key:_____   Answer Given_____
Key:_____   Answer Given_____
Key:_____   Answer Given_____
Key:_____   Answer Given_____
Key:_____   Answer Given_____
Key:_____   Answer Given_____
Key:_____   Answer Given_____
Key:_____   Answer Given_____
Key:_____   Answer Given_____
Key:_____   Answer Given_____
Key:_____   Answer Given_____
Key:_____   Answer Given_____
Key:_____   Answer Given_____
Key:_____   Answer Given_____
Key:_____   Answer Given_____
Key:_____   Answer Given_____
Key:_____   Answer Given_____
Key:_____   Answer Given_____
Key:_____   Answer Given_____
Key:_____   Answer Given_____
Key:_____   Answer Given_____
Key:_____   Answer Given_____
Key:_____   Answer Given_____
Key:_____   Answer Given_____
Key:_____   Answer Given_____
Key:_____   Answer Given_____
Key:_____   Answer Given_____
Key:_____   Answer Given_____
Key:_____   Answer Given_____
Key:_____   Answer Given_____

Key:_____   Answer Given_____

Key:_____   Answer Given_____

Key:_____   Answer Given_____

Key:_____   Answer Given_____

Key:_____   Answer Given_____

Key:_____   Answer Given_____

Key:_____   Answer Given_____

Key:_____   Answer Given_____

Key:_____   Answer Given_____

Key:_____   Answer Given_____

Key:_____   Answer Given_____

Key:_____   Answer Given_____

Key:_____   Answer Given_____

Key:_____   Answer Given_____

Key:_____   Answer Given_____

Key:_____   Answer Given_____

Key:_____   Answer Given_____

Key:_____   Answer Given_____

Key:_____   Answer Given_____

Key:_____   Answer Given_____

Key:_____   Answer Given_____

Key:_____   Answer Given_____

Key:_____   Answer Given_____

Key:_____   Answer Given_____

Key:_____   Answer Given_____

Key:_____   Answer Given_____

Key:_____   Answer Given_____

Key:_____   Answer Given_____

Key:_____   Answer Given_____

Key:_____   Answer Given_____

Key:_____   Answer Given_____

Key:_____   Answer Given_____

Key:_____   Answer Given_____

Key:_____   Answer Given_____